Under the Ground

Written by Karen Anderson   Illustrated by Wade Shotter

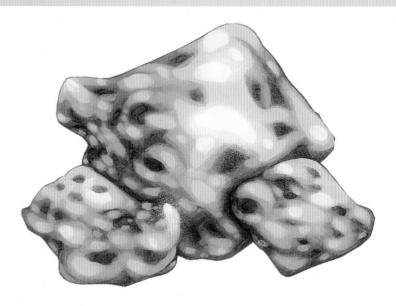

There is gold
under the ground.

2

There is coal
under the ground.

3

There is water
under the ground.

4

There are bones
under the ground.

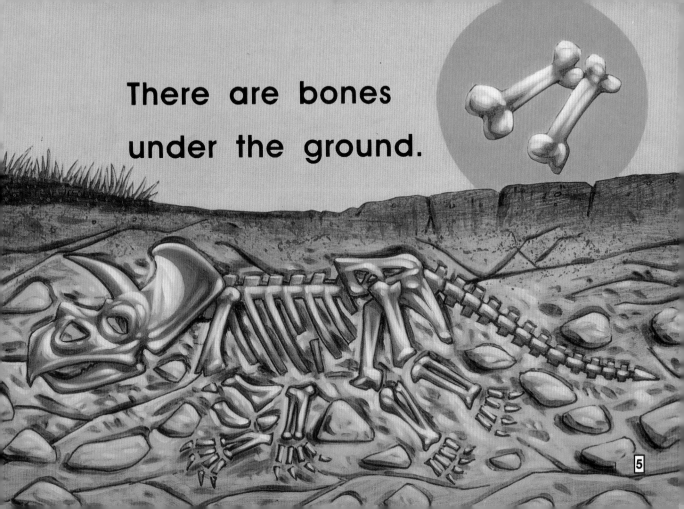

There is lava
under the ground.

6

There are caves
under the ground.

7

There are homes under the ground.